C000121654

BLUSH

Jack Robinson (a pen-name of Charles Boyle, editor of CD culture)
is the author of, most recently, *An Overcoat: Scenes from the Afterlife
of H.B.* and *Robinson*. Nicholas Lezard, *Guardian*: 'I can't think of a
wittier, more engaging, stylistically audacious, attentive and generous
writer working in the English language right now.'

Natalia Zagórska-Thomas is a visual artist, art conservator
and curator. She owns the studio and exhibition space Studio
Expurgamento in Camden Town, London. Ana Maria Pacheco:
'Natalia Zagórska-Thomas is an artist whose work responds to issues
of the contemporary world with wit, intelligence and immense
sophistication.'

Images here are not illustrations, nor are texts captions: they arrived
here together through talk, which is sallies and parries and all
measure of misunderstanding. For technical help with the images,
many thanks to Dr Jens Schaumann.

STUDIO
EXPURGAMENTO

Blush

text   Jack Robinson

images   Natalia Zagórska-Thomas

 CB *editions*

First published in 2018 by CB editions
146 Percy Road London W12 9QL
www.cbeditions.com
in association with Studio Expurgamento
132D Camden Street London NW1 0HY
www.studioexpurgamento.com

Printed in England by Mixam, Hertfordshire

ISBN 978-1-909585-28-7

She was glad that she was alone, for she could feel her face, her throat, even the tops of her arms burning, and she went over to a looking-glass and studied with great interest this strange phenomenon.

   – Elizabeth Taylor, 'The Blush'

'What embarrasses you? Tell me. Do you even know?'

   – Philip Roth, *Deception*

A chink, a gap, a little slippage between me and the other me, the one I'm performing – where the blush gets in.

You cannot tuck a blush behind your ear for later. You cannot buy a blush or steal or borrow one, you cannot swallow or bottle a blush or send one to bed without supper. You cannot invest your (or anyone else's) life savings in a blush. You cannot stamp on a blush until its little light goes out. You cannot lose a blush, or go looking for one. You can post a picture of a blush on social media and you can blow lightly on someone else's blush, to cool it, and you can sweet-talk a blush but you cannot toss a blush up in the air and catch it. You cannot twiddle with a blush, as you might do with loose strands of your hair. You cannot ignore a blush, though you can pretend to. You cannot even read or interpret a blush with any degree of accuracy, it has a life of its own.

A blush is more of a question than an answer. Not a statement, even a tentative one. An exclamation, an ejaculation? (Havelock Ellis, following the American psychologist G. Stanley Hall, suggested that 'the sexual blush is a vicarious genital flushing of blood, diverted from the genital sphere by an inhibition of fear'.) A bewilderment. A panic button.

I cannot see my own face. Unless I'm looking in a mirror or taking a selfie, I cannot see myself blush. Of course I do know when it's happening – warmth and a tingling in the cheeks, a little fluster if I haven't learned to be relaxed about this. There are other parts of body I can't see – the back of my neck, the small of my back, both of those (to me) erogenous zones, not least because they are places my eyes cannot patrol – but the place where my discomfort chooses to display itself is the place that is most visible to others while being invisible to myself. Nor is my discomfort's choice of colour accidental – Julian Bell: 'Red is for sound reasons the most powerful of chromatic cues for attention.' Never underestimate a blush's sense of humour.

Like laughter or weeping or a scream or a grimace or a yawn or fainting or a woman becoming wet or a man getting an erection, blushing is an involuntary physical response to a sensation so immediate and strong that the mind alone cannot cope and says to the body, Here, *you* deal with this.

In school in my early teens, when a teacher asked a question to which I knew the answer I didn't put my hand up because people would look at me and I'd blush. And then I blushed anyway, just thinking about this. And then people did look at me, and I blushed even redder: a loop.

I blushed for confusion and I blushed because I blushed, because blushing was a girl thing and boys were not supposed to. I was ambushed by my own body. I wanted to exact revenge; attempting to take control, I became anorexic.

Later, when buying condoms in Boots, I thought I'd be less likely to blush in front of the woman (invariably) who checked them through at the till if I also bought toothpaste and a pack of Elastoplast and sort of slid them all together. This too didn't work.

A blush hurts – not like a fist to my jawbone, but enough to remind me I'm still alive. A blush is a quick-motion bruise. A blush is a passing wound, subcutaneous, the blood seeking release but the skin holding tight. The heart races.

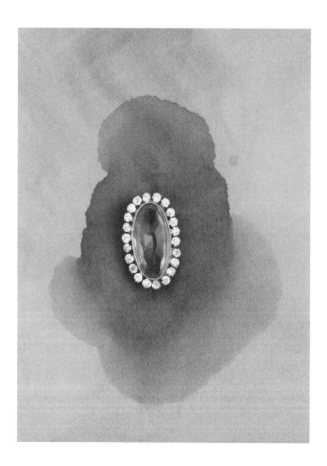

'Is it possible to blush in the dark?' Georg Christoph
Lichtenberg asked, and went on to state that while we can go
pale with fear in the dark, we do not blush: 'For we go pale
on account of ourself, but we blush on account of ourself and
another . . .' Lichtenberg was wrong: certainly we can blush in
the dark. But he was right about blushing being an essentially
social activity. The extreme self-consciousness associated with
blushing entirely depends on awareness of others: a blush
begins in empathy.

Is it possible to blush without the cheeks going red? Denise
Riley posits a kind of 'verbal blush' that occurs when you sense
that you are being asked to adopt 'new habits of speaking that
make you highly uneasy': you want to join in the conversation
but you can't, 'for a form of speaking is a form of feeling, and
the feeling doesn't ring true'. Unsurprisingly, verbal blushes
tend to occur during 'vacuous sex talk'.

A blush can feel as if it's about to gobble me up. A blush is
warm. A blush is an index of awkwardness and confusion.
A blush says something and it speaks true, even if its
truth is partial – something about the body and the social
environment in which that body finds itself having to live
and how the mind struggles to cope with all the mixed
messages. It suggests that neither body nor mind can be wholly
domesticated. And as with many common species of songbird
and butterfly, its numbers are in decline.

The moment when, without any calculated manoeuvring, I find myself alone with the most attractive person at the party. The moment when, having shut the door on the way out to buy a pint of milk, I realise I have left my keys on my desk. The moment when, having walked out of the shop with my pint of milk, I realise I haven't paid. The moment when the person on the Tube I've been staring at looks straight back at me. The moment when I realise that *I* am being stared at. The moment, probably around mid-day, when what happened last night comes back to me in all its grisly detail. The moment when, having avoided being knocked over by a bus by a matter of millimetres, I realise that could so easily have been the end, but isn't. The moment when I realise that I've sent an email to a person for whom it was *not* intended. The moment I am given a present and told I must open it now, in the presence of the giver. The moment when I'm caught with my hand in the till, or my trousers down. The moment when I realise that what I've just said proves I'm not so aware of my own privilege as I'd like to believe I am. The moment I realise I'm older than I thought, and hurry on. The moment when, after I have died, I open my eyes: *this* I had not expected.

The moment *before* the moment registers, before I get it – that nanosecond between the thing happening and me clocking *what* has just happened. That infinitesimal gulp: between the end of one and the beginning of another era.

Replace the full stops with blushes – the common-or-garden kind, the blushes of embarrassment.

In *Keats and Embarrassment*, Christopher Ricks notes that the word embarrassment didn't acquire its modern meaning until the late 18th century; he argues that in the following century 'blushing and embarrassment came to be thought as crucial to a great many social and moral matters', and then asks 'Is not embarrassment not only a nineteenth-century sentiment but a narrowly English one?' Yes, he believes: 'There is indeed something very English about the great importance accorded to embarrassment, and this is part of that deep Englishness of Keats in which he delighted and which is so vital and honourable.'

A History of the World in 100 Blushes, #37. In the dining room of a hotel in a provincial town in England in the late 1950s, my mother calls the waiter over to our table and sends our plates back – the food is barely warm. My mother is recently widowed, and I'm pretty sure she has never done this before; she lacks confidence and is visibly embarrassed. I, aged around six or seven, am embarrassed both for and by her. People are looking. I blush. There *is* something English about all this, not least because class is in the mix here as well as gender, but there is also something (Englishly?) embarrassing about any claim that embarrassment is something the English do better than others (as there is too about promoting tolerance and individual liberty, etc., as 'British' values, as if they were on a par with Cheddar cheese).

At the same time that embarrassment acquired its modern meaning the novel was getting into its stride. In one of its early and still dominant guises, the novel is a tool for investigating how individuals react to the pressures of their environment, for playing off desires and aspirations against social codes, and in the process many blushes and a lot of high comedy are released. Here is Laurence Sterne conjuring a blush out of a trick of the light in *A Sentimental Journey through France and Italy* (1768):

> It was a fine still evening in the latter end of the month of May – the crimson window-curtains (which were of the same color of those of the bed) were drawn close – the sun was setting, and reflected through them so warm a tint into the fair *fille de chambre*'s face – I thought she blush'd – the idea of it made me blush myself – we were quite alone; and that superinduced a second blush before the first could get off.
>
> There is a sort of pleasing half guilty blush, where the blood is more in fault than the man – 't is sent impetuous from the heart, and virtue flies after it – not to call it back, but to make the sensation of it more delicious to the nerves – 't is associated. –
>
> But I'll not describe it. – I felt something at first within me which was not in strict unison with the lesson of virtue I had given her the night before. – I sought five minutes for a card – I knew I had not one. – I took up a pen – I laid it down again – my hand trembled – the devil was in me.

Stendhal's Julien Sorel in *Scarlet and Black* (1830) is an ambitious upstart, the son of a village carpenter who gains employment first as a tutor to the children of a local worthy and his much younger wife and then as a secretary in the household of a marquis in Paris (who happens to have a daughter aged nineteen who is intelligent, proud, beautiful and bored). Julien's progress – a continuous negotiation between hormones and unfamiliar social codes, between sex and class – is ripe for embarrassment at every stage. There are blushes . . . 'Madame de Rênal's face was close to his own, he could smell the perfume of a woman's summer attire, so astounding a thing to a poor peasant. Julien blushed deeply.' 'It was precisely as a young workman, blushing to the whites of his eyes, hesitating outside the door of the house and not venturing to ring the bell, that Madame de Rênal delighted most to picture him.' 'He blushed deeply when speaking of his poverty to a person who was so rich.'

On Julien's first arrival in the town of Besançon – where two hundred pages later he will be condemned to death for the attempted murder of Madame de Rênal – there is a low-key scene in a café in which first a waitress blushes when she takes his order for coffee and bread, then Julien blushes when he tells her he admires her, then the waitress blushes again as she takes his money, counting out his change 'as slowly as she could'. A single blush is being passed from one person to another and back again; it becomes a flirtation.

In Stendhal's *Lucien Leuwen* (1894, posthumous), how does the woman Lucien loves know that he is in love with her?
'He began by falling off his horse twice under my windows . . .'

The first horse that Stendhal himself mounted as a soldier bolted and left the road. Later, in a memoir, he wrote that he had lived 'a life of falling in love and off horses', and in his novels episodes of the latter feature as a regular stage in the progress of the former. In *Scarlet and Black* Julien Sorel – while imagining himself 'a superior horseman' – takes a tumble in the rue du Bac; hearing his account of the incident, the woman he admires 'tried in vain to stifle a peal of laughter'. In *Lucien Leuwen*, the first time Lucien falls off his horse he 'turned red and did his best to look unconcerned'. After the second fall, he believes he is fated to forever appear ridiculous in the eyes of '*cette jeune femme*' who is watching him. In *The Charterhouse of Parma*, Fabrizio has difficulty with horses even before he falls in love: on the battlefield of Waterloo his first horse is a nag that refuses to gallop; his second jumps into a canal and is then stolen from under him: Fabrizio 'was passed over the rump of the horse, then allowed to slide down to the ground, where he fell sitting'.

Falling from a horse is both painful and (to the observer) comic, and it draws attention to itself. In Stendhal, it's a metaphor for the blush that accompanies the clumsiness caused by emotions too strong for the mind to steer; or come-uppance, as on the cheeks of a man who has been too cocksure.

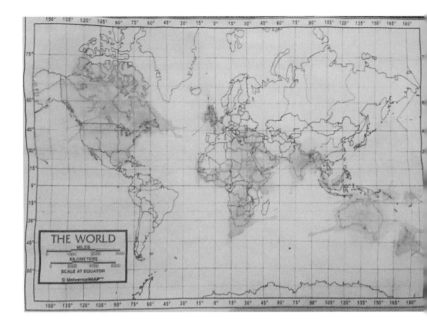

Also during this period – embarrassment coming to the fore, the novel gaining momentum – a blush was playing merry hell on maps of the world over a quarter of the world's land surface, the colour of the British Empire. In Tennyson's *Maud* (1855), male sexual conquest is celebrated as an ever-expanding imperial blush: 'When the happy Yes / Falters from her lips, / Pass and blush the news / Over glowing ships; / Over blowing seas, / Over seas at rest, / Pass the happy news, / Blush it thro' the West; / Till the red man dance / By his red cedar-tree, / And the red man's babe / Leap, beyond the sea. / Blush from West to East, / Blush from East to West . . .'

Another blush from *Scarlet and Black*, on Mathilde's cheeks as she speaks about Julien: 'He has a strong and inborn sense of the differences of social position. It was I, I admit, with a blush, to my best friend, and never shall such an admission be made to any other, it was I who one day in the garden pressed his arm.'

In the marriage market, a woman's blush signified a virtuous reputation; that it had an erotic allure, suggesting sexual feeling under restraint, was a bonus. This little dance was based on men being physically stronger than women. Here, a different pattern of power applies: Mathilde has been born into a social class far superior to Julien's. Bored by her regular suitors, she takes the initiative herself; and still blushes.

'Rose coloured slightly; but she gaily laughed.' This is Rose Armiger, Henry James's 'Bad Heroine' in *The Other House* (1896), one of several characters named Rose in fiction by 19th-century men. Rose wears a white dress and carries 'a showy red parasol'. Rose loves a man who has promised to his dying wife that he will never remarry while their child is alive. Rose kills the child.

In Maupassant's story 'Rose' (1884), two young women take part in a flower parade in Cannes and then ride in their coach to the next bay along the coast. The sun is setting, the calm sea melting into the horizon: it's a perfect evening, lacking only '*un peu d'amour*'. Without love, Margot says, life is unbearable; Simone declares she would rather not be loved at all than loved by, for example, the driver of their coach tonight, or a household servant. Margot then relates her experience with a maid she hired four years previously, a story within the story which unsettles the tranquil summer evening.

Rose, the maid, is tall, a little pale and very shy – she rarely speaks, and blushes often ('*toujours un peu rougissante*'). She can sew, embroider and dress hair. Margot comes to regard her more as a companion than a servant; she enjoys being dressed and undressed by Rose, scarcely feeling the touch of her fingers, and after her bath she allows Rose to towel her dry and massage her as she lies on her sofa. And then one day a police inspector arrives and tells Margot that she is harbouring an escaped prisoner. After all the other servants have been seen, Rose is summoned and is immediately arrested. Rose is a man; Rose is also a convicted rapist and murderer. Margot says she feels no anger at having been deceived but rather, when she thinks of the unknown woman who was raped, a deep sense of humiliation.

Maupassant has a blush-pink variety of rose named for him.

In August 1862, twenty-two years before Maupassant's story, another maid called Rose died in Paris of tuberculosis. Rose Malingre had served the Goncourt brothers for a quarter of a century, and on the day she dies they write in their journal of their grief: 'She shared everything with us, our sorrows and our joys . . . Our bodies, in sickness and in health, were accustomed to her attentions. She knew all our habits, and she had known all our mistresses.' A week later, they discover that Rose had led a life unknown to them, a life of 'dreadful orgies, nights out, sensual frenzies'. She drank, had children out of marriage, stole money and food for her lovers. The Goncourts are 'filled with a great commiseration for her, but also with a great bitterness': 'Suspicion of the entire female sex has entered our minds for the rest of our lives: a horror of the duplicity of woman's soul, of her prodigious gift, her consummate genius for mendacity.'

First, Rose is made the object of an intolerable idealisation: kind, loyal, long-suffering, intimate but without making any demands. Then, when the Goncourts discover that Rose has appetites, they turn on her – and not just her, but 'the entire female sex'. What's suspicious here is the neatness of the reversal, and the way 'suspicion' has entered the minds of both the brothers equally, as if they were not independent adults with minds of their own but confused and angry children. *Spoilt* children. (A lover of one of the Goncourts tells him: 'You look like a little boy staring at a jam sandwich.')

When Jules Goncourt died of syphilis in 1870, his brother packed roses from their garden around the corpse before the coffin lid was screwed down.

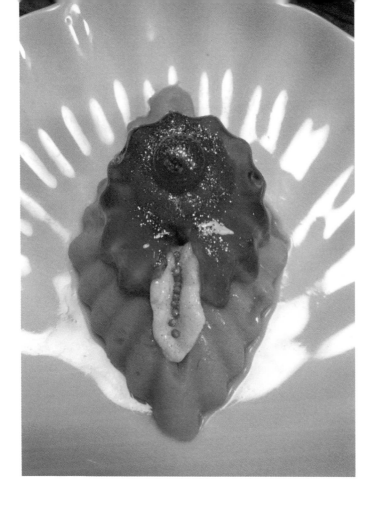

'I rolled a hoop with her when I was a boy,' writes one of the
Goncourts of the good Rose, before she changed into the bad,
'and she brought me apple turnovers at bridges.' Ah, Rose –
you surely knew from the Book of Genesis that a woman who
offers apples to a man is making herself vulnerable, and that
whatever happens next she is always going to get the blame.
Don't look at *me*, says Adam to God: 'The woman whom thou
gavest to be with me, she gave me the fruit of the tree.'

Darwin: 'Women blush more than men.' Because the narrative of shame – who gets to feel it, who doesn't – is written by men.

Darwin: 'The blind do not escape. Laura Bridgman, born in this condition, as well as completely deaf, blushes.'

Darwin considered blushing 'the most peculiar and the most human of all expressions'. He asked his network of correspondents to inform him about 'blushing in the various races of men', 'how far down the body blushes extend', and whether those confined to asylums for the insane ever blush. 'Mr Geach informs me that the Chinese settled in Malacca and the native Malays of the interior both blush. Some of these people go nearly naked, and he particularly attended to the downward extension of the blush . . . I am assured by Gaika and by Mrs Barber that the Kafirs of South Africa never blush; but this may only mean that no change of colour is distinguishable.' (Darwin's many other interests included orchids, bees, the mental development of young children, and worms: 'Worms have played a more important part in the history of the world than most persons would at first suppose.' There are times I want to hug this man.)

'The mental states which induce blushing', according to Darwin, 'consist of shyness, shame, and modesty'. All of these are socially conditioned. As Martha Gellhorn noted when she was approached in West Africa by a group of laughing women wearing nothing but a few leaves, 'Modesty is certainly a weird and various human quality.'

Shyness, shame, modesty and embarrassment are often all in the bag together. In an identity parade, it can be hard to narrow down and say, *That one*.

Shyness and modesty have to do with why we (some of us) blush when we receive praise, but shame is in there too. We have been found out, and found wanting. We don't really believe that we deserve praise, and we suspect that whoever is doing the praising knows this too, and everyone else. We are wearing the emperor's new clothes, and even these are a bad fit.

Embarrassment is shame-lite. Embarrassment has to do with manners, clumsiness, getting tangled up in etiquette. (Darwin: 'The rules of etiquette always refer to conduct in the presence of, or towards others. They have no necessary connection with the moral sense, and are often meaningless.') Shame is heavyweight. The high priests have invested in it. Shame functions as an apparatus of social control, particularly of women.

When it suits them – when this strategy can be a means of retaining power – the high priests can change the rules. Shame used to be attached to several aspects of life from which it has now largely, but far from completely, been detached. Divorce, for example. Illegitimacy. Abortion. Sexual orientations that differ from what was once cemented in law as the 'norm'. Or debt: formerly, if you got into debt you went to prison; now, the young are encouraged to go to university and become massively in debt before they even start earning. Shame still attaches to poverty (unclaimed means-tested benefits amount to many billions per year); and also, in internalised ways, to illness, depression, being bullied . . . In sexual matters, the #MeToo movement is a long-overdue attempt to reverse the allocation of shame, shifting its burden from those without power (generally women) to those with power (usually men); the patriarchy may be so deeply embedded that it's unlikely to crack open very soon, but it's a start.

Herr Cazotte, in Isak Dinesen's *Ehrengard* (1963), does not mind being celebrated as a Don Juan as well as a portraitist because the right to seduce is his privilege as an artist, and the manner in which he exercises it demonstrates his fine feeling: with certain women, 'the smile, the side glance, the waltz or the tears' may be all he requires. With Ehrengard, he ponders for some time what act will best reveal 'the fine fleur of her being'. He makes his decision: 'In the blush.'

Cazotte discovers that Ehrengard bathes naked in a nearby lake in the early morning. He will paint her, nude but with her face averted, and exhibit his painting in a gathering of courtiers and connoisseurs with Ehrengard by his side and she, recognising herself, will 'blush into a deep exquisite crimson, a mystical *rose persan*'. This will not be 'the blush of offended modesty' – 'To the mind of the artist the very idea is blasphemy' – but a blush in which 'her past, present, and future will be thrown before my feet. She is to be the rose which drops every one of her petals to one single breath of the wind and stands bared.' And then Cazotte will leave her, 'intact but annihilated'.

The plot twists: a pregnant princess goes into hiding, a duke becomes suspicious, a child is kidnapped – whose? In a scene of dramatic confusion, Ehrengard claims that the child is hers, and that 'Herr Cazotte is the father of my child.' Though the word is not spoken, she is accusing him of rape. A normal man, the storyteller remarks, knowing the combative reputation of the man Ehrengard has promised to marry, 'might have gone white, even white as death' – 'But Herr Cazotte, who was an artist, blushed': 'His brow and cheeks, all on their own, radiated a divine fire, a celestial, deep rose flame, as if they were giving away a long-kept secret.'

Changes in the rules don't take effect overnight. Not everyone is told that they *have* changed. Very few of the rules are actually written down: they are learned from the behaviour of others around us as we grow up. KEEP OUT notices are rarely necessary; children internalise boundaries without even knowing what's being fenced off.

The shame narrative is governed by power. When money makes a grab for absolute power – when greed is given the green light and the accumulation of money is switched from being a means to an end to an end in itself – you have an inversion described by James Buchan as 'the greatest to have occurred in the moral sentiments of the West'. Miserliness loses its stigma and becomes 'the condition of moral health'. Moral choices are simply 'bought out'. Friendship, love, honour – all trumped by money.

Blushes in big business are rare to the point of invisibility. As long as money is being made, lying and dodgy deals and low-level corruption are reckoned par for the course. Very few shareholders turn up to AGMs. Blushes are rare in politics too; many people don't bother to vote.

Sport has its own confusions. To maintain a perceived difference from big business (which high-level sport *is*), sport has to appear to still adhere to notions of fair play and level playing fields (those fields were never, ever, level), and the punishments for breaking the rules have to be harsh. In early 2018 a member of the Australian cricket team was caught ball-tampering on camera. (Ball-tampering: roughing up the surface of the ball to make it swing in the air when bowled. Small margins.) Two senior players were implicated, and both broke down in tears at press conferences – not because they'd been cheating but because they'd been *caught* cheating. Honour survives as a ghost that slumbers off-stage while a lot of cheating (and getting away with it) goes on, waking up only when the cheating gets found out.

A story about – let's call her – Megan Jones, who at the age of seventeen returned one morning from the cowshed to the kitchen of the farm on which she lived with a blush on her cheeks; and when her mother asked whether the boy from the neighbouring farm had been around to help with the milking, she said no; and the blush was still evident when her father came home, and when she woke on the following morning, and in fact did not fade over the following years, and neither did the tingling sensation in the girl's cheeks. Her father was ashamed of his daughter for having brought shame on the family. The girl was compelled to a diet of milk and greens, and to sleep with cold compresses on her cheeks, and was bled with leeches, but to no avail. Her mother understood that she would never be blessed with grandchildren. The congregation of the local chapel called upon the bishop to perform an exorcism. Curious travellers made their way to the farm from as far as London. After Megan's father fell from a ladder and died she attended his funeral, her face concealed by a veil, but this was the only occasion in eight years on which she was seen in public. In 1830, aged twenty-five, Megan Jones left the farm in secret but voluntarily, touching the cold stones of the wall by the track down to the road for luck. Nothing is known of her further life.

There are other stories, always. The one about the woman who never blushed, not once in her whole life. The one about the manly blush. The one about the king who promised his daughter in marriage to the man who blushed deepest.

Shamelessness plc. To stimulate economic growth, shamelessness is put out to tender. The allocation of shame – previously a national resource managed according to a jumble of traditions of the kind that are shuffled together to inform the British (unwritten) constitution – is awarded on license to successful bidders, thereby ensuring that it is efficiently targeted to productive ends and less is wasted in sexual and other non-profit enterprises. The government assures all hard-working families that they have nothing to fear: as long as they continue to buy lots of things they don't need, don't get ill and don't carelessly lose their homes or their minds, they won't notice any difference. Oh, and buy stuff – did we mention that? Shares in insurance companies rise steeply.

As shame shifts and taboos crumble – and every-which-way
sexual fantasies become available for viewing online, click and
click again – is there anything left to be embarrassed *about*? As
a man boasting about grabbing women 'by the pussy' is voted
into office as US President and a racist unfunny clown who
refers to non-white people as 'picaninnies' is appointed to be
the UK's Foreign Secretary – and all this wheels by, wheels
by in the news-feed – has even the capacity to be embarrassed
atrophied? As privacy is surrendered to corporations and
public agencies that track our online clicks and record our
street-life on surveillance cameras – and this data is 'harvested'
(that bucolic ring) and packaged and sold on, and on again –
and the odds against our being *found out* are diminishing to
zero – do we even care?

If embarrassment is 'a nineteenth-century sentiment', as
Christopher Ricks suggested, blushing may be a sort of
residual leftover, like the curtsy or the bow.

Goo, poo, mud, mess: the tactility of the world.

In the beginning, the private – soft, squidgy, protected by no hard shell – is barely separate from the public. Very gradually, as infants become children, they learn which things are OK to put in your mouth and which are not. And which things, and words, are OK and which are not OK to come *out* of your mouth. And they learn how to interpret and manage the public world through social codes that are at least as strange as the things they claim to codify.

Is her spit decent if it's in her mouth? Yes. (This is nine-year-old Kully questioning Herr Krabbe in *Child of All Nations* by Irmgard Keun.) And if she spits on the table? No – neither her nor her spit. And the word 'spit' itself? 'Saliva' might be better. So if she spits her *saliva* on the table? Still indecent. But if the word itself is decent but not the thing, what makes a word indecent? (Once, you'd know a word was indecent if your mother promised to wash out your mouth with soap if she ever heard it again.) Kully: 'Sometimes I'm not sure whether I don't understand grown-ups, or if they're just too stupid for words.'

The English codes relating to sex are especially odd. Once upon a time, many (most?) white middle-class boys acquired their first knowledge of what a woman's body looks like – and no knowledge at all about how it actually functions – from the photographs of women on nudist beaches in *Health and Efficiency* magazine or the tabloids' Page 3 girls in their pathetically tiny range of staged poses. The *Carry On* series of films – 1958–78, me aged from seven onwards – was not just silly but damaging. Gilbert Adair: 'the eroticism of the series has jammed at the fundamentally infantile stage of *disclosure*, in which nudity is a (never quite attained) culmination, rather than a point of departure'. Denise Riley: 'There seems to be something particularly and depressingly British about the blend of prurience with babyishness.' Embarrassment about sex in those films was *built in*.

How did girls acquire knowledge of the male body? From medical textbooks, edited by esteemed male doctors? From Michelangelo's *David*, with his bunched-up little penis? But art books are expensive and no more helpful than the Page 3 girls. And help *is* needed. For a long period in polite middle-class history, girls were not supposed to know about sex but also somehow assumed to know, just by being girls: a knowing not-knowing (Rumsfeld territory here: known unknowns and unknown knowns).

Tony Judt: 'The life of an early-'60s adolescent male was curiously confined. We still inhabited our parents' moral universe . . . There was a well-founded presumption of innocence and ignorance, for boys and girls alike . . . Back then we all lived on Chesil Beach.'

Childhood is not innocent but is often presumed to be a stage of life in which we were more true to ourselves than the compromised beings we've ended up becoming. Some security questions asked as back-up when we forget our passwords and have to choose another: What was the name of your first pet? What is the name of the street where you grew up? What was your childhood nickname? What is the name of the first person you kissed? Those were the days.

Gilbert Adair: 'I remember that, at summer school, sharing a bedroom for the first time in my life, I would demurely sit on that side of my bed which faced away from my room-mate's when removing my underpants.' 'I remember never quite knowing, in my relationship with the French, when – or how – to switch from "vous" to the more familiar "tu".' 'I remember not properly understanding the significance of the expression "blow job" and believing it to mean that one's sexual organs were breathed over (an idea which, I have to say, I found extremely stimulating).' 'I remember, as a teenager, quite regularly shoplifting sweets from Woolworths.'

I remember being caught shoplifting a magazine and thinking that the shopkeeper was letting me off with some stern words because I was blushing so deeply. But then, he was never really going to go to court over the theft of a literary magazine priced at just 9 pence (pre-decimal currency). With me seen off the premises, he was going to laugh aloud.

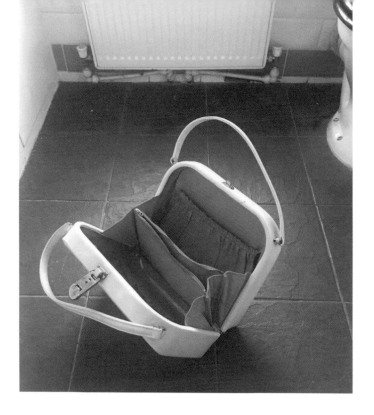

Darwin: 'The young blush much more frequently than the old.' Because to live in a state of continuous confusion is neither mentally nor physically sustainable, and after adolescence a settlement between the private and the public is negotiated. Deciding roughly who we are (or accepting the decision of others) and binding this in with routine and habit is a survival mechanism.

Adolescence is Early Modern: superstition and fairy tales and comfort blankets still boiling in the pot together with all the new ingredients, discovery of the world and scientific enquiry and the body suddenly going a bit wild. The gas is on high. Of course the cheeks get hot.

Keats's poems, Christopher Ricks notes, 'are full of blushes' – as they are too of swellings, quiverings, oozings, seepings. These are all forms of trespass: refusals to be contained by a given line.

In 'The Eve of St Agnes', Madeline is described as she undresses as 'Half-hidden, like a mermaid in sea-weed' – and for Ricks the sea-weed 'epitomizes the central strength and sanity of Keats's erotic poetry': sea-weed, both the word and the thing, 'arouses strong mixed feelings; it is both fascinating in its tactile pungent oddity and yet faintly repellent', and 'It is the incorporation, within the large apprehension, of this faintly embarrassing possibility of response that makes Keats's poetry at once truthful and generous.' Elsewhere, Ricks praises for similar reasons Keats's use of the words 'gummy' – 'so attractive and yet tacky' – and 'sluicy'.

Ricks: 'The case for a great deal that is best in Keats is that space for adolescence; or rather for a recognition of those insights into life which may be more accessible to a perceptive adolescent than to others.'

After adolescence, there are bills to pay, jobs to be found, commitments to be made. After adolescence, blushing becomes less frequent (some pharmacological stimulation might help: a pill, please). After adolescence, the pressure is on to appear as if we know how to behave.

We do have *some* idea, but we are lost, basically. We live on the cusp of ignorance and oblivion. The world is a mystery. We don't know other people – know them well, know them fully – and we don't know ourselves and our knowledge of other species is barely more than zilch. We don't even know how many species there *are*. We don't even know, most of us, how our computers and smart phones and satnavs work, let alone our televisions and fridges: as at a societal level technological know-how increases, so at an individual level does ignorance. (Trotsky in the 1930s: 'A hundred million people use electricity and still believe in the magic power of signs and exorcism.') We know precious little about love and about history and about what it is to be born and to die, and the little that we do know we are very bad at passing on to others. We don't know how to organise ourselves and run things decently, we barely know how to walk down the street, and whatever embarrassment prompts our blushes is essentially embarrassment at our not-knowing, along with a vague feeling that for reasons we can never properly spell out we are somehow *in the wrong*.

The final quotation in Ricks's *Keats and Embarrassment* is from a letter dated 24 October 1818 in which Keats (aged twenty-two) writes of meeting a woman he admires in Covent Garden – 'I passed her and turned back – she seemed glad of it' – and asking if he can walk her home. She agrees – 'and then again my thoughts were at work what it might lead to'. In her living room the woman is friendly and hospitable; she gives Keats a grouse to cook for supper for Tom, his brother who is ill. Because Keats has 'warmed with her before and kissed her', he is aware now, in the present moment, that to kiss her again and not to kiss her again are *both* potentially embarrassing, and for both himself and the woman. He goes for it. The woman refuses him – 'not in a prudish way but in as I say a good taste – She contrived to disappoint me in a way which made me feel more pleasure than a simple kiss could do – she said I should please her much more if I would only press her hand and go away.' They part as friends.

If the flutter of a butterfly's wings in one continent can set off a tornado in another continent, then allow that a blush is not just decorative.

Or, presumably, the burp of a rat, the fart of a pig, but a butterfly is prettier. A blush *is* decorative. It's pink. It's a rush of blood. It's cute as a butterfly and it is vulnerable to its own appeal.

It's by my face – there it is in my passport and on my driving license – that I am recognised and identified in public. I glance in the mirror: observer and observed, two in one, the register a bit askew.

In embarrassment, head down and hands to cheeks, shielding, protective – a movement as involuntary as the blush itself.

Young children, covering or closing their eyes, can believe they are not being seen.

Or a mask – as in carnival, when the world is turned upside down and the everyday rules don't apply. Or a veil – because the face is the centre (in Havelock Ellis's phrase) 'of anatomical modesty'.

We didn't have an altarpiece in the house where I grew up but in my mother's bedroom there was a dressing table with triptych mirrors and little drawers for unguents.

Cosmetics conceal as well as display. Here is Thackeray in *Vanity Fair* (1848) on Becky Sharp, after one of her little lies has been found out: 'She rubbed her cheek with her handkerchief as if to show there was no rouge at all, only genuine blushes and modesty in her case. About this who can tell? I know there is some rouge that won't come off on a pocket-handkerchief; and some so good that even tears will not disturb it.'

The Golden Age of blushing may be said to have ended in 1894, the date of first publication (in *The Yellow Book*) of Max Beerbohm's essay 'The Pervasion of Rouge': 'The era of rouge is upon us, and as only in an elaborate era can man, by the tangled accrescency of his own pleasures and emotions, reach that refinement which is his highest excellence, and by making himself, so to say, independent of Nature, come nearest to God, so only in an elaborate era is woman perfect. Artifice is the strength of the world, and in that same mask of paint and powder, shadowed with vermeil tinct and most trimly pencilled, is woman's strength.'

Saturated with irony and making parodic use of traditional rhetorical strategies, Beerbohm's essay parades its own artifice.

In 'The Pervasion of Rouge', Beerbohm rejoices that the old days are over, the days when women were 'utterly natural in their conduct – flighty, fainting, blushing, gushing, giggling and shaking their curls. They knew no reserve in the first days of the Victorian era.' Not content with 'rinking [skating] and archery and galloping along the Brighton Parade', they 'sped on . . . from horror to horror': 'The invasion of the tennis courts and the golf links, the seizure of the bicycle and of the typewriter, were but steps preliminary in that campaign which is to end with the final victorious occupation of St Stephen's [the House of Commons].' By great good fortune, 'Artifice, that fair exile, has returned', and 'the horrific pioneers of womanhood who gad hither and thither . . . are doomed.'

Artifice's first requirement of women is that they should 'repose': 'With bodily activity their powder will fly, their enamel crack. They are butterflies who must not flit, if they love their bloom.' There is more: since 'expression is but too often the ruin of a face', 'the safest way by far is too create, by brush and pigments, artificial expression for every face'. For the Reformed Toilet Table, Beerbohm proposes 'a list of the emotions that become its owner, with recipes for simulating them'. According to her skill with cosmetics, a woman 'will blush for you, sneer for you, laugh or languish for you' – monotony will be banished, 'And for us men matrimony will have lost its sting.' This is just the beginning; science, harnessed to pleasure, will soon so work its magic that even 'Arsenic, that "greentress'd goddess", ashamed at length of skulking between the soup of the unpopular and the test-tubes of the Queen's analyst, shall be exalted to a place of consummate honour upon the toilet-table of Loveliness.'

By 1904 the tattooist George Burchett was inflicting 'permanent delicate, pink blushes on ladies' cheeks'. The word tattooing was not mentioned; the ladies underwent 'a minor surgical operation' in a Mayfair salon staffed by 'lady assistants dressed in the sombre uniforms of hospital nurses' and furnished with aspidistras, dwarf palms, a large divan 'draped with a gorgeous Chinese silk rug' and a lacquered table with the required instruments: 'the tattooing tool, a cut-throat razor, a box with cotton wool and a few small jars containing dyes'. The ladies 'were brave and grateful'. Journalists were invited to attend demonstrations (which employed 'a girl from Soho, or a chorus-girl from a music hall who was treated free of charge'). *The Tatler*: 'A chaste and charming blush'. The *Daily Mail*: 'The rosy cheeks that rival Nature at her best . . .'

Since the late 19th century the blush has been coarsened: marginalised, cosmeticised, monetised, medicalised . . . While many novelists have employed the blush as a device to explore ambiguous psychological states, the currency has more usually been debased. Pasted like emojis into the plots of traditional romance fiction, blushes add a light sexual frisson. Blushes are Mills & Boon and Barbara Cartland (whose heroines were described by a *Times* reviewer as 'helpless, coy, game-playing blushing violets who say no and run away, no matter what they feel'). Blushes are 'bashful', 'virginal', 'maidenly'; they have been co-opted into a reactionary system of binary gender stereotypes: pink for girls, blue for boys.

Blushing is not cool. It is associated with social anxiety, which undermines self-esteem, and the consequent feelings of inadequacy can be horrible, but the implication in the titles of self-help books that social anxiety is somehow abnormal and needs to be corrected is stupid. Social anxiety is as normal as it gets. For those who suffer at the extreme, surgery is available: endoscopic thoracic sympathectomy, which involves cutting the nerves that cause facial blood vessels to dilate and can result in increased sweating in other parts of the body.

A blush is a flag of inconvenience, a busted flush, a gulp, a glitch, a stammer, a flutter, a flinch.

On the cheeks of a a retired dentist (65), stuck in traffic on the M25; of a woman (33) whose daughter has gone missing in Tesco's in Sunderland; of an ex-soldier (42) who fought in the Gulf War, while watching a late-night TV documentary; of an apprentice stylist (19) sweeping the floor of a hairdessing salon in Hertfordshire; of a stand-up comedian (23) whose punchline is not funny at all; of a banker (49) in the gents at the Guildhall, noticing the virulent yellow of his pee; of a girl (9) who has just been awarded second prize; of a chambermaid (27) in a luxury hotel, on opening the door of room 429; of a man (89) with cancer of the throat, in his bed in a basement room; of a woman (48) at a bus stop, looking into her handbag; of a boy (16) who has tripped and fallen; of a porn star (25) collecting his pay cheque; of a waiter (29) who is attempting to carry at least one too many dishes; of Robinson (?), standing in the rain at the edge of a car park. The Democratic Republic of Blush.

A blush brings to the surface – the cheek! – emotions that are impure and imprecise. Own them. A blush expresses something that isn't communicated in the verbatim transcript and certainly not in the press release. The blush is a social mechanism whose purpose is obscure and perhaps it's best that way, because awkwardness and not-knowing are what make it (Darwin) 'the most human of all expressions', though I don't want to be dogmatic about this. I'm not trying to *sell* the blush.

In the concluding section of Virginia Woolf's *To the Lighthouse* Lily Briscoe sets up her easel on the edge of the lawn 'as a barrier, frail, but she hoped sufficiently substantial to ward off Mr Ramsay and his exactingness'. The man is respectable and also desolate, bad-tempered, self-pitying. He approaches Lily ('ruin approached, chaos approached') and attempts to engage her in conversation. Lily resists, a wall of silence, until Mr Ramsay notices that his boot-laces are untied, and Lily too looks at his boots and involuntarily praises them and Mr Ramsay, holding one foot in the air, is off – a monologue about his glorious boots, concluding with a lesson in how to tie laces. And then: 'Why, at this completely inappropriate moment, when he was stooping over her shoe, should she be so tormented with sympathy for him that, as she stooped too, the blood rushed to her face, and, thinking of her callousness (she had called him a play-actor) she felt her eyes swell and tingle with tears?'

Lily's blush is a flash – painful in its abruptness – of empathy: not knowledge of who Mr Ramsay is or what he is feeling except in the most fugitive of ways, and certainly nothing *useful* ('He tied knots. He bought boots. There was no helping Mr Ramsay on the journey he was going'), but a vision of Mr Ramsay not occluded by herself – a vision immediately succeeded (because the self-effacement exacted by awareness of the otherness of others cannot be borne) by an an intense self-scrutiny. Children appear on the terrace and Mr Ramsay slings a bag over his shoulder and they are off to the lighthouse, that stupid lighthouse, and it is all too late, and Lily is left feeling 'a sudden emptiness; a frustration'.

In *Mrs Dalloway* Woolf offers the blush as an image for just such a fleeting form of knowledge, or intuition. Mrs Dalloway reflects that she is often the recipient of another woman's confession of 'some scrape, some folly' – 'And whether it was pity, or their beauty, or that she was older, or some accident – like a faint scent, or a violin next door (so strange is the power of sounds at certain moments), she did undoubtedly then feel what men felt. Only for a moment; but it was enough. It was a sudden revelation, a tinge like a blush which one tried to check and then, as it spread, one yielded to its expansion, and rushed to the farthest verge and there quivered and felt the world come closer, swollen with some astonishing significance, some pressure of rapture, which split its thin skin and gushed and poured with an extraordinary alleviation over the cracks and sores! Then, for that moment, she had seen an illumination; a match burning in a crocus; an inner meaning almost expressed. But the close withdrew; the hard softened. It was over – the moment.'

Mid-afternoon on a weekday in March 2023 in the City of London: half an hour after a thunderous shower of rain the sky turns unaccountably pink, as if a wind has blown north from a red desert, carrying sand of such fine grain it is barely material, and with the light a silence. Something is happening that nobody knows how to speak about, something awful but also releasing, but into what?

The markets get the jitters. Traffic slows, as around the scene of an accident. On the pavements, pedestrians step carefully around pink puddles.

Someone is reminded of something but cannot remember what (something biblical, something in a dream?). Someone confesses to their partner that they have been leading a double life for years and the partner says, *You think I don't know?* Someone runs a hot bath. Someone pours a triple whisky. Someone sings a song they didn't even know they knew the words to. Someone tells another someone they love them and someone else makes rapid use of the office shredding machine. Someone goes out to buy a sandwich and is never seen again. Someone sees God. Someone unlocks a drawer and stares dully at what is inside. Someone phones their mother for the first time in twenty years and someone else throws a brick through a shop window. Someone carries on working, head down. Someone takes a sleeping pill, and a few more to make sure. Someone laughs, someone cries.

The pinkness in the air fades, dissolves or becomes transparent. A meteorologist with sideburns is interviewed on the 10-o'-clock news and the markets pick up. The puddles evaporate.

IMAGES

Front cover *Self Portrait in Kid Gloves*, pastel on photocopy paper, 2018
Facing title page *Pins and Needles*, mixed media with sewing pins, 2014
page 1 National University, Kiev, Ukraine, iPhone photograph, 2016
   3 National Museum of Art, Krakow, Poland, iPhone photograph, 2015
   4 *Insomnia*, mixed media with pillow, 2011
   6 *Stain*, Camden Town, London, iPhone photograph, 2016
   8 Northern Line, London, iPhone photograph, 2017
  12 Warsaw, Poland, iPhone photograph, 2016
  15 *The World*, gouache on photocopy paper, 2018
  16 *Figurine*, mixed media with lipstick case, 2014
  17 *Jabot*, mixed media with kid glove, 2014
  18 Rose, St Martin's Gardens, London, 2018
  21 *Valentine's Jelly*, edible sculpture, 2014
  22 *Untitled*, mixed media with doll's head, 2018
  25 *La Solida . . .*, Malaga, Spain, iPhone photograph, 2008
  28 Brick wall, London or Athens, iPhone photograph, 2016
  31 St Martin's Gardens, London, 2018
  32 Pavement, Camden Street, London, 2018
  37 *If you don't like pink . . .*, iPhone photograph, 2018
  41 Confetti, King's Road, London, iPhone photograph, 2017
  43 *Stitch in Time*, mixed media with button hole, 2016
  44 *Remnant*, mixed media with horse hair, 2014
  46 *Rose Damask*, detail, iPhone photograph, 2017
  48 *Suteryna*, Camden Town, iPhone photograph, 2018
  52 Dusk, London, iPhone photograph, 2017
  57 *Cheek by Glove*, crayon on photocopy paper, 2018

TEXT REFERENCES

Edmond and Jules de Goncourt are quoted in the translation by
Robert Baldick (*Pages from the Goncourt Journals*, NYRB, 2007);
Maupassant in the translation by H.N.P. Sloman (*Boule de Suif and
Other Stories*, Penguin, 1946); Stendhal in translations by G.K. Scott
Moncrieff (*Scarlet and Black*, Everyman, 1938), John Sturrock (*The
Charterhouse of Parma*, Penguin, 2006) and H.L.R. Edwards (*The
Green Huntsman* and *The Telegraph* [Books 1 and 2 of *Lucien Leuwen*],
John Lehmann, 1951).

Gilbert Adair, *Myths & Memories* (Fontana, 1986)
Max Beerbohm, 'The Pervasion of Rouge', in *The Works of Max
 Beerbohm* (Dodd, Mead, 1922); first published in 1894 as
 'A Defence of Cosmetics'
Julian Bell, https://www.theguardian.com/artanddesign/2009/
 jun/13/modern-art-colour-chart
James Buchan, *Frozen Desire: An Inquiry into the Meaning of Money*
 (Picador, 1997)
George Burchett, *Memoirs of a Tattooist* (Oldbourne, 1958)
Charles Darwin, *The Expression of the Emotions in Man and Animals*
 (1876), excerpted in *The Portable Darwin*, ed. Duncan M. Porter
 and Peter W. Graham (Penguin, 1993)
Isak Dinesen, *Anecdotes of Destiny and Ehrengard* (Vintage, 1993)
Havelock Ellis, *The Evolution of Modesty*, in *Studies in the Psychology of
 Sex*, Vol. 1 (F. A. Davis, 1923)
Martha Gellhorn, *Travels with Myself and Another* (Eland, 1982)
Tony Judt, *The Memory Chalet* (Penguin Press, 2010)
Irmgard Keun, *Child of All Nations* (trans. Michael Hofmann,
 Penguin, 2009)
Georg Christoph Lichtenberg, *The Waste Books* (trans. R. J.
 Hollingdale, NYRB, 2000)
Christopher Ricks, *Keats and Embarrassment* (OUP, 1974)
Denise Riley, *Impersonal Passion: Language as Affect* (Duke University
 Press, 2005)

You cannot rush a blush. You cannot vanish a blush by flicking a switch. A blush has little idea of why it's here but now it's at the party it is both quick and reluctant to leave, and I know that feeling. I stay in my seat in the dark as the credits scroll by, bunching up my knees to let other people past while I clock the names of the gaffers, best boys, wardrobe assistants and caterers. A book I've enjoyed stays around for a while on a chair or a table before I shelve it. After I've said goodbye and closed the door and come back into the room where the plates and the wine glasses are still on the table and the voices are still in the air: *that* time. When you switched off a cathode-ray-tube TV, a little dot would appear on the screen and I'd watch until it faded to blank. I don't want to go to bed.

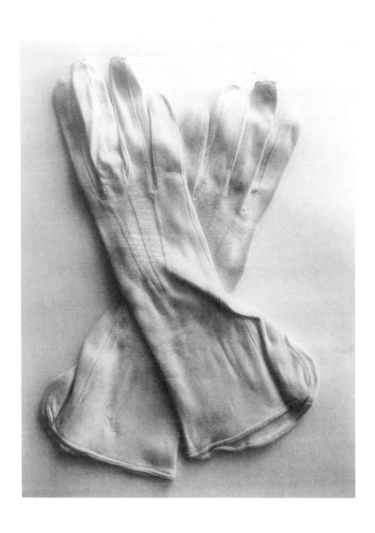

Since 2012, artists shown by Studio Expurgamento (www.studioexpurgamento.com) have included Andrzej Maria Borkowski, Sophie Herxheimer, Bryan Illsley, Ti Parks, Paula Rego, Danuta Solowiej, Almuth Tebbenhoff and Helen Wilks.

Since 2007, writers published by CBe have included Will Eaves, Gabriel Josipovici, Agota Kristof, Lara Pawson, Francis Ponge, Christopher Reid and Diane Williams. Books can be ordered from www.cbeditions.com.